"It helps now and then to step back and take a long view.

The Kingdom is not only beyond our efforts,
it is beyond our vision.
We accomplish in our lifetime only a fraction
of the magnificent enterprise that is God's work.
Nothing we do is complete, which is another way
of saying that the kingdom always lies beyond us.
No statement says all that could be said.
No prayer fully expresses our faith.
No confession brings perfection, no pastoral visit
brings wholeness.
No program accomplishes the Church's mission.
No set of goals and objectives include everything.
This is what we are about.
We plant the seeds that one day will grow.

We water the seeds already planted
knowing that they hold future promise.
We lay foundations that will need
further development.
We provide yeast that produces effects
far beyond our capabilities.
We cannot do everything, and there is a sense
of liberation in realizing this.
This enables us to do something,
and to do it very well.
It may be incomplete, but it is a beginning,
a step along the way, an opportunity for the Lord's
grace to enter and do the rest.
We may never see the end results, but that is the
difference between the master builder
and the worker.

We are workers,
not master builders.
We are ministers,
not messiahs.
We are prophets of
a future not our own."

"A Future Not Our Own"

by Bishop Ken Untener

in honor of

Saint Óscar Arnulfo Romero y Galdámez

THE REDEMPTIVE NONPROFIT

A PLAYBOOK FOR LEADERS

TABLE OF CONTENTS

FIRST PRINCIPLES

The nonprofit organization is a recent development in history; organized charity, service, and outreach are not. In the West, for much of the last two thousand years, charity was the work of local Christian congregations, or simply individuals and households, serving their neighbors in need. But around the time of the Industrial Revolution, in the English-speaking world, this charitable work began to be channeled through organizations distinct from the church itself, responding both to new chasms of inequity and to the increasing complexity of urban, industrial society.

It was not until the turn of the twentieth century that these charitable efforts were granted a special legal status, leading to an explosion of charitable "nonprofits." Today, there are over one million public charities in the U.S., with a vast array of missions and strategies, from small neighborhood-focused groups to those operating on a global scale. The sector as a whole accounts for more than 5% of U.S. GDP and roughly 10% of wages.[1]

[1] http://nccs.urban.org/data-statistics/quick-facts-about-nonprofits

Outside the U.S., especially in low- and middle-income countries, the nonprofit sector (including multinational and U.S.-based charitable work) has a disproportionate economic footprint, in some cases surpassing the local public and private sectors.

But when it comes to delivering social good, especially to those in the most need, many nonprofits fall short in impact and integrity, in spite of the noble goals for which they are organized (and for which they receive favorable tax treatment).

When we hear this, our minds may go immediately to the aging nonprofit hobbled by inefficiency and mediocrity—or to high-profile cases of charities that have become notorious for misusing donor funds. But while these stereotypes may dominate the popular imagination about nonprofits, they don't represent the great opportunity for transformation in the sector.

Indeed, the nonprofit world is thick with disciplined, ethical, and creative leaders. Many are capable of scaling visionary organizations with widespread impact; others are endowed with the persistence to focus on a single community for the long haul. Yet many of these leaders and organizations fall short of the durable impact they hope to deliver.

Some do more harm than good, not out of corruption or incompetence, but out of well-intentioned mindsets and actions that fail to properly account for the complexity of the human condition.

Even in the most effective, resourceful, high-growth nonprofits, we often settle for practices and norms that are necessary but insufficient for the outcomes we seek. We may focus on numbers of people served, size of budget, retained donors, and great stories—knowing that these are inadequate proxies for measuring our true impact. We propose that there is a higher horizon of opportunity for the redemptive nonprofit, one that seeks the renewal of the larger society as well as all the stakeholders involved in the work.

The starting point, we believe, is to contend with two fundamental vulnerabilities built into the nonprofit structure. We've labeled these the "stakeholder gap" and the "nobility trap."

The stakeholder gap is a *structural* issue. Often, the nonprofit's funders do not require its services, and those who receive its services are not its primary funders.

The people in the best position to assess whether the organization is actually creating value—its beneficiaries, the ones who would be the "customers" of a for-profit business—are not the same people who deliver the financial resources that all modern nonprofits need to survive.

While this gap between donors and beneficiaries does not apply to the same extent to all tax-exempt organizations (many of which, such as prestigious arts organizations, raise their principal funding from their own "customers"), it applies dramatically to those with the seemingly most noble missions. The more vulnerable an organization's beneficiaries are, the less likely it is that they are the ones who provide it financial feedback and accountability for results.

The nobility trap is a *human* issue stemming from the admirable intent of the leader and the organization. Nonprofits begin with the ostensible purpose of serving others and making the world a better place; and most people assume that nonprofit leaders and team members are making sacrifices relative to other more lucrative or prestigious career options. All this can be true—but it can prevent the leader and organization from being held to the highest standards of excellence.

In the worst case, sentimental admiration for a leader or cause can lead to neglect of the scrutiny that would disclose the gaps between an organization's stated mission and its own beneficiaries' assessment of its impact.

Because these two vulnerabilities arise from the very purpose of the nonprofit structure, and because very few leaders set out to take advantage of them, it is easy to treat them as benign. But amplified by our human tendencies toward pride and self-justification, they lead to blind spots that can cause any nonprofit to do unintentional harm, and to miss opportunities for significant impact.

Without intentional and sustained countermeasures, nonprofit leaders are likely to fall into creating internally divided organizations, where board, donors, staff, and beneficiaries are siloed from one another. Over time, the leadership team learns to carefully control the narratives and relationships that cross the gaps between audiences. Strategy is defined with fewer key stakeholders in the room; donors may be offered only the success stories and kept out of the true challenges of the mission, or given too much rein to define the problem and the solution.

The communities served by the nonprofit may feel their voices are stifled.

These divisions complicate the already difficult prospect of translating lofty intent into sustainable beneficial impact. Though everyone is in favor of personal, communal, and structural transformation, these are very hard to measure, prove, or repeat. As a result, many nonprofits and their donors settle for powerful stories and input metrics alone, avoiding the difficult and essential work of impact modeling, structured listening, monitoring, evaluation, and reporting.

The nobility trap also leads directly to the all-too-common nonprofit with an inspiring mission but a toxic culture—where staff are underpaid, overworked, and flounder with little direction or wither with insufficient autonomy; where vendors learn to anticipate zero-sum negotiations, unrealistic expectations, and late payments; where boards are reluctant to contain the influence of a charismatic leader; where donors sense they are being manipulated; and where potentially beneficial partnerships are avoided or suffocated through suspicion and turf wars.

THE CUMULATIVE RESULT IS THAT THE VERY SECTOR MANY PEOPLE CONSIDER TO BE THE MOST GENEROUS ACTUALLY FACES THE GREATEST RISK OF BEING THE MOST EXPLOITATIVE.

But it doesn't have to be like this. In this playbook, we want to encourage nonprofit leaders to chart a different course, on two fronts. First, recognizing that the stakeholder gap and nobility trap foster mediocrity (or even unwitting exploitation) in strategy and management, it lays out some essential elements of excellent nonprofit organizational practice.

More significantly, it aims for a redemptive rethinking of the very premise of the modern nonprofit. The practice of excellence is necessary but insufficient to repair the fundamental flaws in the way we channel our charitable activities. Something deeper is needed—something that recognizes dignity and agency among those we serve by restoring the relationships that were the original, personal heart of God's vision for just charity.

This kind of nonprofit work depends upon sound ethics and best practices, but it goes beyond them. The commitments and practices in this playbook can be implemented in organizations without a particular faith commitment, but they are rooted in a distinctly Christian view of human beings and our shared purpose in the world, which are summed up in the term "redemptive."

THE REDEMPTIVE FRAME

The Christian account is that human beings are more frail and sinful than we would like to admit, but capable of more possibility and glory than we often are willing to imagine. Each of us is infinitely worthy, yet none of us can perfect ourselves. Likewise, nature and culture were created very good, have become distorted through abuse, and cry out to be restored, yet they cannot be put fully right through our human efforts.

In fact, putting the world right—bringing about personal, spiritual, social, cultural, and environmental healing and restoration—is God's great purpose in history, into which we believe we all are invited.

The pattern of restoring glorious yet broken things to their rightful state, even at great cost, is best described using the word *redemption*. This economic term (to buy back something or someone and return it to its proper condition) is used repeatedly in Scripture to describe Jesus' work of paying with his life so that human beings could be restored to a right relationship with God and his creation.

WE BELIEVE WE ARE TO FOLLOW THE CORE REDEMPTIVE PATTERN OF **CREATIVE RESTORATION THROUGH SACRIFICE** IN OUR LIFE AND WORK.

In the Praxis community we are committed to a way of practice that we call redemptive entrepreneurship: sustained and ambitious improvisation on this redemptive act of creative restoration through sacrifice, in the realms of venture creation and funding, organizational leadership, product and service design, process innovation—or any endeavor in which we take risk to bring about true flourishing for all people.

Redemptive entrepreneurship is a form of *praxis*—faith in action—where we express our love of God and neighbor through the ventures we build and lead.

We use The Redemptive Frame to connect our personal vocation and leadership behavior to our organization's work in the world; and to explore opportunities for the greatest redemptive impact of that work.

THE REDEMPTIVE FRAME DESCRIBES THE DIMENSIONS OF A NONPROFIT OR ANY KIND OF VENTURE:

The Strategic Vision consists of everything the venture sends into the world to embody and express the mission, in the form of products, services, programs, brands, narratives, and physical spaces.

The Operating Model consists of the venture's culture, functions, assets, business models, and partnerships that develop and deliver the Strategic Vision into the world.

The Leadership Intent consists of the motives, worldviews, and practices of the leadership team, whose decisions and actions set the course for the venture's Strategic Vision and Operating Model.

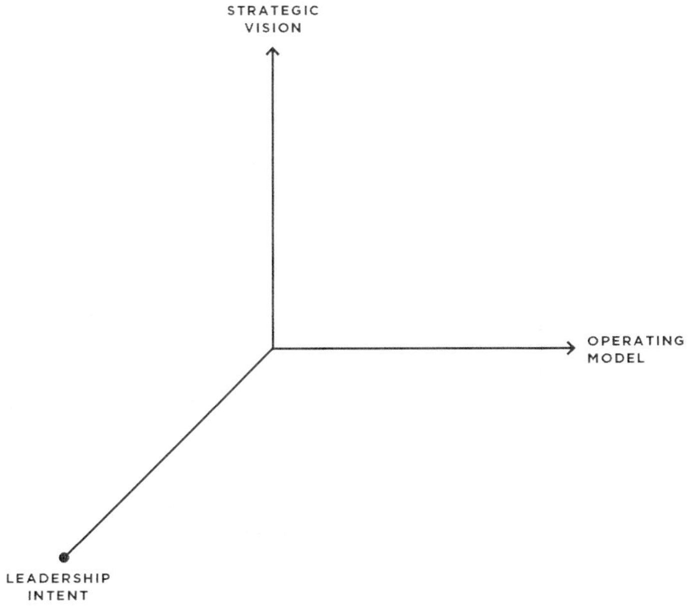
STRATEGIC
VISION
OPERATING
MODEL
LEADERSHIP
INTENT

THE REDEMPTIVE FRAME ALSO ADDRESSES HOW VENTURES AND THEIR LEADERS APPROACH THE WORLD:

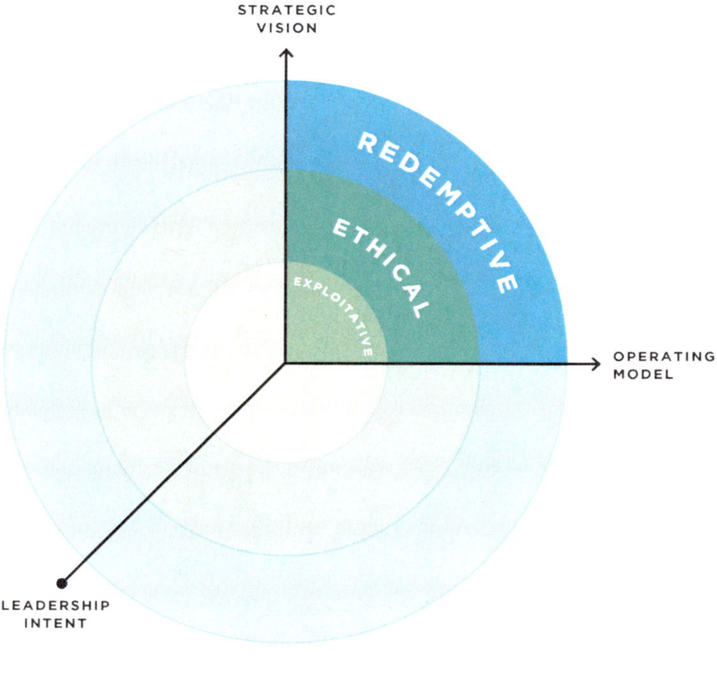

The people and ventures following the Exploitative way do whatever it takes to win. They pursue every opportunity to take advantage, to extract value at others' expense, to tilt and optimize all things in their favor, to leverage the letter of the law, to suppress or amplify truth to gain an edge.

Its doctrine is *"Win at Any Cost."*

The people and ventures following the Ethical way reject the Exploitative, and instead seek to do good through their work. They want to address problems, do no harm, operate fairly, create sustainable value, be morally enlightened, raise the bar, win clean, and improve the world.

Its doctrine is *"Doing Good and Doing Well."*

The people and ventures following the Redemptive way also seek to do good through their work. Yet they push beyond the Ethical, even inverting it in places—seeing the world as broken and in need of God's ultimate renewal; recognizing all persons as God's image-bearers, worthy of blessing; and knowing themselves as fallen and in need of grace.

Its doctrine is *"Creative Restoration Through Sacrifice."*

EACH DIMENSION PROGRESSES FROM EXPLOITATIVE TO REDEMPTIVE:

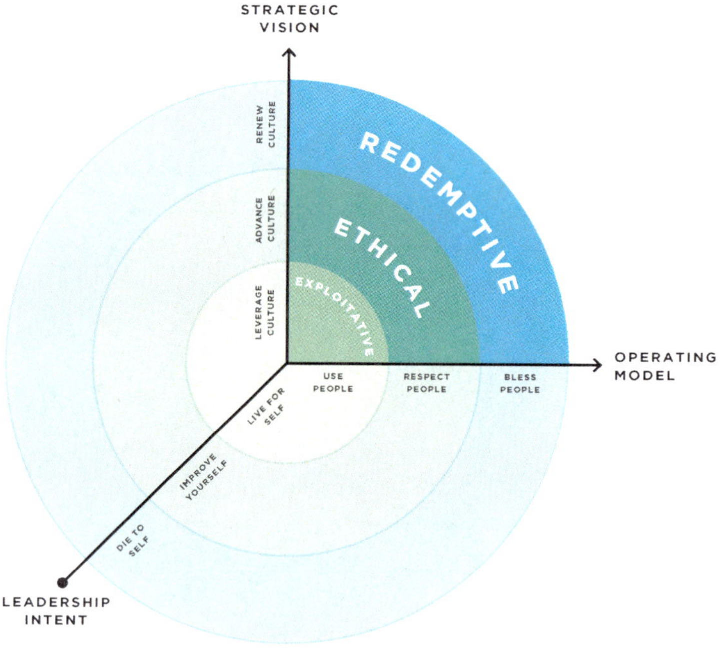

The Exploitative venture originates from a leadership team that lives for self. They will likely lead the venture to leverage culture for their benefit, and to use people as resources to expend on the mission.

The Ethical venture originates from a leadership team seeking to improve themselves. They will likely lead the venture to advance culture for the better, and to respect people in and around the venture.

The Redemptive venture originates from a leadership team seeking to die to self. They will likely lead the venture to renew culture as God is renewing all things, and to bless people through the venture.

A Redemptive Strategic Vision is a way of designing and leading the venture as a culture-making force to join God in the renewal of all things. It is grounded in a commitment to create beautiful and humanizing products, services, and spaces, backed by truthful and God-honoring brands and narratives.

A Redemptive Operating Model is a set of processes, culture, and systems that bless people within and beyond the venture. It involves designing and building virtues like grace, generosity, justice, and patience into workforce practices, interactions with customers, partners, and funders, and use of capital.

A Redemptive Leadership Intent is the fusion of ambition, talent, discipline, and insight with wisdom, spiritual maturity, stewardship, and dying to self. It comes from identity, motives, imagination, and practices that are submitted to God and seek first the good of others.

REDEMPTIVE STRATEGIC VISION
REDEMPTIVE NONPROFIT
REDEMPTIVE OPERATING MODEL
REDEMPTIVE LEADERSHIP INTENT

A REDEMPTIVE IMAGINATION FOR THE NONPROFIT SECTOR

We hope to inspire a new generation of leaders to go beyond the baseline of ethics and excellence that should characterize any organization (whether or not it receives a tax exemption)—to building nonprofits that embody the radical hope of the Christian gospel and its power to transform persons, communities, and the course of history.

We believe that through communities practicing redemptive work, we will see a resurgence of nonprofits that do not use faith or good intentions as an excuse for subpar performance. These organizations will promote flourishing for people and places not adequately served by the market, while working against the exploitation of all stakeholders—beneficiaries, donors, employees, volunteers, and partners.

If this vision is consistently and creatively lived out, we will see transformation in the nonprofit sector.

It can become an even more productive ecosystem where diverse voices and actors are brought together, unified in pursuit of solutions to the world's most pressing issues. Leaders of redemptive nonprofits can be set free from the fruitless attempt to serve multiple masters; they will experience the joy of rebuilding relationships across cultural differences that never should have been severed in the first place.

PERHAPS MOST SIGNIFICANTLY, IN THE PROCESS OF SERVING ALONGSIDE ONE ANOTHER, ALL OF US—NOT JUST THE "TARGETS" OF OUR MISSION FOR CHANGE—WILL EXPERIENCE REDEMPTION AND RESTORATION.

SIX COMMITMENTS OF THE REDEMPTIVE NONPROFIT

STRATEGIC VISION

We live and tell an integrated story, resisting the urge to craft a misleading or oversimplified narrative. Our story has many actors, and is always being written in active partnership with those closest to the work.

We base our mission on a theologically informed theory of change, designing and evaluating programs with significant leadership from the communities we serve, and in active partnership with others in our field. We practice proximity and collaboration in our programs, resisting the temptation to shape our work from a comfortable distance.

OPERATING MODEL

We develop a leadership team that will outlast the current generation, rejecting the pattern of overdependence on one charismatic leader.
We cultivate talent by developing each person for and beyond their contribution to the mission, instead of treating them solely as organizational resources.

We invest relationally in a healthy, engaged board, refusing to treat governance as a necessary evil. We pursue active unity and diversity within the board, ensuring that all stakeholders are represented and that expectations are high, clear, and mission-aligned.

We build mutually transformative relationships for the people who provide funding for our work. We confidently approach potential donors as whole persons who may be called to join the mission, rather than solely as funders upon whose resources we depend.

LEADERSHIP INTENT

We surrender our identity to God and our ambition to the good of our neighbors. Instead of acting as though we own the organization, we practice the mindsets and habits of stewardship, using our position to advance others' glory and fullness rather than our own.

STORY

WE LIVE AND TELL AN INTEGRATED STORY

SUMMARY

We live and tell an integrated story, resisting the urge to craft a misleading or oversimplified narrative. Our story has many actors, and is always being written in active partnership with those closest to the work.

OUR REALITY

The genesis of every nonprofit is a story—a protagonist, a problem or injustice, a witness, a spark of empathy, a vision for change. Over time, many of these stories intertwine and evolve into an organizational narrative that propels vision, programs, teams, and resources into reality.

But as nonprofits and leaders endeavor to live out our public story, we are under so much pressure to be (or to seem) more than we are.

We see needs in the world and can hardly live with incremental change (especially when the change other organizations promise seems so swift and dramatic). So we simplify the problem and over-promise on what our solution will accomplish. We promote simple success stories, create unrealistic expectations, and become subservient to a vision we were never capable of fulfilling.

The truth is that all nonprofit work is slower than we care to admit, fraught with ups and downs, progress and setbacks. Deep change can come from the work we do, but rarely does it emerge in a linear, evenly distributed fashion—so it cannot be easily or accurately represented in an email or 90-second video, a simple ratio on an assessment website, or an annual report.

Too often, we "rewrite the roles" of the people we serve as we tell the organization's story. The need to tell a crisp story tempts us to make larger claims than are currently true. The messy reality can be compressed, polished, and stretched into oversimplified stories of impact. Despite our best intentions, beneficiaries may become used instead of honored; and donors may also become unwitting accomplices as they encourage and support our work without being able to see our stories in context.

Instead, we long to use our creative gifts to tell the truest version of our story rather than the grandest.

PRACTICES

1. We are truthful and transparent with all constituencies—board, donors, beneficiaries, the public. Though we must vary emphases, modes of communication, sequence, and level of detail according to the audience and context, every version of our story aligns with the truth as we know it.

2. We are fiercely truthful about both the ambitious possibility of the mission and the limitations and obstacles that we will likely face. We root out hyperbole from our communication, instead using modesty and balance—for example, reporting good news as "progress" rather than as "success," and reporting progress and setbacks in tandem with one another. We openly acknowledge failure, naming what we have learned without spreading blame.

3. We elevate the stories of the people we serve, honoring them as image-bearers with shared humanity and agency. We platform those closest to the mission as its chief protagonists and storytellers—highlighting their successes, sharing their names, and inviting them to read and contribute to our communications.

4. While we aim always to honor people, we steer clear of romanticism and sentimentality in our story, avoiding positive stereotypes just as much as negative ones. Instead, we celebrate steps of genuine progress in the communities we serve, and refuse to overstate the role our work has played in their lives.

5. We tell our organizational story with many heroes, including other agencies and actors, without overreliance on the unique genius or call of any person or group. We actively solicit and celebrate the successes and contributions of others and resist elevating our organization by speaking negatively of others.

THE GOOD NEWS

Mark Twain once jotted in his notebook, "If you tell the truth, you don't have to remember anything." In this spirit, a commitment to integration and truth in organizational communications is liberating. It sets us free from having to maintain multiple narratives about ourselves and our work. It deflates the temptation to manipulation and exploitation that comes with all cause-driven storytelling—even when we see others in our sector doing those very things. We shed the stress of trying to fulfill unrealistic promises, and the distortion in mission and core values that can creep in as we try to fulfill them.

We will learn to celebrate the smaller points of progress along the way; we will build muscles for expecting, managing, and learning from failure. We won't rein in our ambition for what we can collectively do to address social ills and brokenness, but our ambition will remain rightly matched with our capacity. In the long run, this will actually greatly increase our organizations' and our societies' capacity for real and lasting change.

When we use storytelling to empower and dignify those we serve, we give them ways to celebrate small but real progress with us, setting both them and us free from the anxiety of needing to impress outsiders with a "success story" that we know is only partially true.

Nonprofits can become known as the greatest truth-tellers. We have a front-row seat to the most broken and the most beautiful parts of human experience. No inflation of that story is necessary. There is both human and God-inspired drama in this work, and if we can commit to being truthful to everyone around us about what we see and experience, we will open the doors for them to journey through the challenges to see the good, the true, and the beautiful.

PROGRAMS

WE PRACTICE PROXIMITY AND COLLABORATION IN OUR PROGRAMS

SUMMARY

We base our mission on a theologically informed theory of change, designing and evaluating programs with significant leadership from the communities we serve, and in active partnership with others in our field. We practice proximity and collaboration in our programs, resisting the temptation to shape our work from a comfortable distance.

OUR REALITY

Every nonprofit has two headwaters: need and hope. We see a gap in existing structures and institutions and become convinced that someone must rise to the challenge of filling that gap. And we come to believe and hope that we have identified effective ways to make a difference. It is out of this initial identification of need and articulation of hope that our mission originally arose, and they remain the most powerful sources of energy for growing and sustaining our work.

Yet to the extent that we begin our work as outsiders, with solutions we hope or assume to be innovative, we often lack the patience and discipline to get proximate, study the complexity of the issues, and make time for mutual learning and cultural understanding. Even those who begin as "insiders" can quickly become distant from their original context. As our programs grow, we are tempted to evade the challenging work of clarifying our mission and testing its assumptions. Did we actually identify the original need correctly? Are the strategies we put our hope in actually effective over time?

This is not to say that we do not develop indicators for our work. But sometimes these are simply the items that are easiest to measure—like budget size, growth rate, and "percent to program"—rather than the ones that best measure our work's actual effect. And because of the stakeholder gap, we often fail to track what matters most to the people we serve. We stop learning, and too easily fall into the rut of complacency.

In the worst cases, we are sufficiently isolated from the complex realities on the ground that we come to believe that our organization is the answer, the missing puzzle piece, to the problem we have identified in the world. We relegate to the background the two most important contributors to our success: those we serve, and the other organizations and actors working on adjacent issues.

Meanwhile, we are tempted to avoid developing and asserting a theory of change for fear that it will reveal complexity in our mission field that we cannot actually control, or demonstrate the incompleteness of our interventions. Even if we have articulated such a theory, we neglect to assess and refine it based on feedback from our (hoped-for) beneficiaries over time. We also can easily neglect to shape, test, and refine our theory of change based on a theologically robust view of human beings and societies, settling for accounts of both problems and solutions that are too thin and neglect social, relational, and spiritual dynamics.

All this makes us more likely to perpetuate programs that support our initial conception of our mission and theory of change, rather than evolving them to meet actual needs—or to chase changing currents of culture and philanthropic fashion.

We prolong dependency on our organizations and fail to create opportunities for leadership from the community. And we may even treat other organizations as competition for resources and success rather than co-laborers for the same cause.

Instead, we long to see our community's need more clearly, and to rekindle our hope that change is not only possible but truly underway.

PRACTICES

1. We seek creative ways to root our work in the communities who know the challenges and opportunities best. Our program leadership includes ever-increasing representation from these communities. We plan, execute, evaluate, and report together through teams that include multiple stakeholders.

2. We define our mission in clear view of our interdependence with other actors and agencies in the community and broader ecosystem. We investigate existing organizations before beginning a new program or service that would fulfill a similar goal, with a bias toward collaboration and open-source learning rather than autonomy.

3. We publish and invite accountability for a theory of change or impact model that tracks how programs facilitate true behavior change and flourishing in those they serve.

4. We invest our time, energy and resources in the programs that generate the greatest outcomes. Our culture of intentional monitoring and evaluation sets the expectation that we will prototype continuously, abandon unfruitful pilots, pivot less-productive programs, and sunset projects that have served their purpose.

5. We develop and affirm (at least internally) a statement expressing the theological vision underlying our mission of restoration and a biblical basis for our theory of change.

6. We routinely investigate and decline attractive opportunities that promise growth but are not essential to our mission.

THE GOOD NEWS

When we are no longer merely interested in the lives of our beneficiaries but become implicated in them, we bridge the stakeholder gap and are more likely to avoid the nobility trap. The closer we are to the communities we serve—physically, relationally, and operationally—the more meaning we and our team will experience in our work. Our learning will be more agile, our insights more reliable, our decisions more fact-based, our partnership more genuine. Though the work may sometimes be slower and more arduous, it will also be more substantive and lasting.

As we collaborate with others, we are set free from the temptation and burden of territorialism—the need to count indicators of success in our field as belonging to us rather than the overall mission of God in the world. Indeed, we are set free from the tyranny of the word our, as if either the problem or the solution belonged to us.

Proximity and partnership mean that we become less satisfied with merely technical or sentimental interventions that lend themselves to superficial metrics.

Our original senses of need and hope will be re-animated through a heightened awareness of the dignity, tragedy, and possibility of human beings and their societies in light of the redemptive power of God.

This deep sense of mission helps us stay the course under conditions of both frustrating setbacks and intoxicating success. Anchored in good news that does not depend on us for its truth or efficacy, we have the endurance and confidence to pursue lasting, restorative change.

TEAM

WE DEVELOP EACH PERSON FOR THE MISSION AND BEYOND

SUMMARY

We develop a leadership team that will outlast the current generation, rejecting the pattern of overdependence on one charismatic leader. We cultivate talent by developing each person for and beyond their contribution to the mission, instead of treating them solely as organizational resources.

OUR REALITY

Every organization intends to attract great people, build a healthy culture, and develop inspiring leaders—yet most organizations fall well short in actual practice, usually beginning with the cultural habits surrounding the founder.

A charismatic leader has a remarkable capacity to inhabit a nonprofit's mission, cast vision, and set into motion a movement of energy, goodwill, and resources. But in our need to sustain that momentum and resource flow, we reinforce the myth that the visionary leader is indispensable to the mission. Each time we rely solely on the leader to deliver the vision, the message, or the funding in the near term, we defer the joyful but painstaking work of developing the next generation of leaders.

Across the team, we treat people as "resources" to be allocated and used rather than as whole persons to be developed and blessed. To limit overhead, we pay staff less than we should and provide inadequate benefits, believing that the mission is important enough that our team should be willing to make unhealthy and unsustainable sacrifices.

Instead of building inclusive leadership pipelines, we mold teams around our leaders' personalities. Or to jumpstart our work, we hire people we believe are "stars," and reward them accordingly, without paying close attention to whether they are actually well aligned with our ethos and mission.

With every passing year, the organization loses talent and resilience. We become known for our lack of excellence, our overworked and discontent staff and volunteers, or both. The remaining leaders can feel—and begin to act—like we work with the leftovers, both in people and in money. The communities and stakeholders we serve also come to tolerate and internalize a narrative of scarcity and mediocrity; and a successful transition to the next generation of leaders becomes less likely.

Instead, we long for our team and its culture to be compelling carriers of our mission.

PRACTICES

1. We build capacity and confidence across the team to counteract the tendency to elevate the importance of one charismatic leader. As part of our culture of developing people, senior leaders regularly invite rising team members to accompany them into important settings and actively "share the stage" in their public appearances.

2. We build and nurture robust diversity—of age, gender, ethnicity, skill set, and experience—at every level of the organization, knowing that these differences lead to greater organizational impact as well as personal transformation. We create inclusive leadership pipelines, making way for women, people of color, and those who have lived experience in the issues we address.

3. We steward people for and beyond the work of the organization. We communicate clear expectations about each team member's role, contribution, and areas for development. We creatively adjust roles and assignments to build competence, broaden capability, and distribute our authority and influence—all in view of both the organization's and the individual's goals.

Where people are not meeting expectations, we communicate and act quickly, first adjusting for better alignment within the organization, and if necessary, guiding and supporting them in leaving the organization.

4. We honor each team member through our human resources practices, including compensation, benefits, and tools that allow us to attract and retain the right talent—and that enable people to commit wholeheartedly to their work in light of all aspects of their vocations.

5. We practice healthy and sustainable work rhythms, including intentional patterns of daily, weekly, and seasonal rest. We encourage leave for fathers, mothers, and caregivers to devote themselves to intensive care for those dependent on them without jeopardizing their long-term prospects with the organization.

6. We celebrate volunteers and creatively honor their contributions to the mission, by adapting each of these practices wherever possible to our interactions with them.

THE GOOD NEWS

Freed from the myth of the "heropreneur,"[2] we leaders can experience the great joy of creating something that will actually outlast us and flourish even more in the future than in the present. Our leadership is guided by our most important performance evaluation: the one that will come several years after we've left the organization.

We hope to see transformation in the culture of the nonprofit sector. It will increasingly be led by healthy, joyful, and balanced persons who ultimately trust that the mission is not theirs to own, but rather to steward for a period of time. They will be rooted enough to offer their fullest selves to the mission, without pouring their whole worth into the rise or fall of the venture. They will hold the organization and its mission with utmost care while also surrendering it to God and to others.

[2] Daniela Papi-Thornton, "Tackling Heropreneurship," *Stanford Social Innovation Review*, February 23, 2016.

Likewise, our team members will joyfully offer their creative best in service to the mission, working within sustainable margins while at peace with the sacrifice that all redemptive action requires.

Even when we feel that resources are insufficient to meet overwhelming needs, we find joy in creatively investing what we have in ways that can produce manifold returns. We trust that God can do more than we could ask or imagine.

Indeed, we have been captivated by the countercultural vision of a banquet where the poor and excluded actually receive the very best of food and drink. We believe the communities we serve, insofar as they are excluded from the world's tables, deserve not just competency but excellence; not just the good but the best. The nonprofit space can increasingly be the employer of choice for many of the most qualified—the place where they can pursue ambition, build careers, and spend a lifetime of fruitful work.

BOARD

WE INVEST RELATIONALLY IN A HEALTHY, ENGAGED BOARD

SUMMARY

We invest deeply to cultivate a healthy, engaged board, refusing to treat governance as a necessary evil. We pursue active unity and diversity within the board, ensuring that all stakeholders are represented and that expectations are high, clear, and mission-aligned.

OUR REALITY

Nonprofit organizations often treat governance as a distraction from the true mission.

If a healthy board could be summed up as high trust plus high engagement, most nonprofit boards are low on one or both attributes. High-trust, low-engagement boards passively assent to the will of the CEO, failing to provide the diverse perspectives, depth of contribution, or committed stewardship of his or her leadership that are essential to the organization's health. CEOs learn to treat this kind of board as a kind of super-volunteer focus group—providing encouragement and input but little other value.

Low-trust, high-engagement boards commonly devolve into factions, each of which sees its role as protecting the interests of their constituents against competing interests; members regard the senior executives or other board members as potential antagonists; and the CEO experiences the board as meddling and counterproductive to the strategy and operations of the mission.

Even in boards with more collaborative intent, members are often unsure of their role and purpose or isolated from organizational realities, and are therefore unable to offer real strategic value or accountability. There is little iron-sharpening or mission advancement within board meetings, and governance is characterized by confusion, anxiety, or passivity.

Instead, we long for our board's guidance and oversight to be among our organization's greatest assets.

PRACTICES

1. In the same spirit of telling an integrated story, we practice transparency and accountability in our governance processes, with no secrets or surprises between the CEO and the board. The CEO and board chair channel the board's productive attention within a spirit of openness to all input. Annually, the board conducts a self-assessment, as well as an evaluation of the CEO. We set clear goals and speak truth in these settings, knowing that a rebuke from a friend is a gift.

2. We cultivate our board members as senior mission leaders. We thoughtfully steward their time and gifts, providing them the information, experiences, clarity, and relationships they need to best serve their role in guiding the mission.

3. The board and CEO lead from a posture of mutual trust, in which the board respects the role of the CEO, and holds him or her responsible for implementing the mission of the organization. They avoid unhealthy direct engagement with other staff members that could cause confusion around the priorities or direction, and instead focus communication through the CEO.

4. We recruit our board to include representation and meaningful influence from all stakeholder groups, including those closest to the delivery of our mission. We refuse to recruit board members who can fill gaps in our expertise or giving capacity but are not aligned with the deepest values of the organization.

5. We cultivate authentic, mutually appreciative relationships across the lines of board, donors, staff, and stakeholders. They work together in programs and public events, and invest time together in private events such as board retreats. We seek creative approaches to ensure that all board members regularly experience and participate in our work.

6. The board takes an active role in the development plan for senior talent, including regular conversations about succession as the organization evolves. The board chair, in particular, carefully attends to the health and sustainability of the CEO in his or her life and work.

THE GOOD NEWS

We hope for abundance as the board faithfully guides the mission and supports and empowers the day-to-day work of the leader. Members will have their own unique, complementary contributions and perspectives; but once a decision is made by the board, they will speak with one voice.

The dangers of the stakeholder gap—making programming decisions from a strategic distance, falsely pitting the expectations of donors against the needs of those we serve—are minimized when meaningful decisions and tradeoffs are guided by a group representing all stakeholders, who are submitted to one another in the mission.

Likewise, an active board guards the organization against the self-congratulation of the nobility trap. Unsatisfied with noble intent alone, they will insist on progress toward impact. They can objectively spot areas where the organization unwittingly exploits by settling for mediocrity or by otherwise taking advantage of people in its programs and practices.

Healthy boards are the principal stewards of the organization's enduring leadership. They objectively focus on the levers necessary to ensure that the organization outlasts each generation of leaders.

The greatest dividend of a board's redemptive presence is its effect on the CEO. There is a sustained power for a leader in the deep assurance that their board is committed to their flourishing and the institution's alike, and will provide both accountability and support toward these ends. They become freer to innovate and take risks, more assured in their mission, less susceptible to blind spots, more likely to share power, and released to rest in the knowledge of God's sovereignty over their life and work.

FUNDING

WE CONFIDENTLY APPROACH DONORS AS WHOLE PERSONS

SUMMARY

We build mutually transformative relationships for the people who provide funding for our work. We confidently approach potential donors as whole persons who may be called to join the mission, rather than solely as funders upon whose resources we depend.

OUR REALITY

Too many donor-nonprofit relationships are marked by asymmetry, alienation, and desperation.

Perpetually anxious for resources and often unwilling to professionalize the fundraising processes and teams that lead to financial durability, nonprofit leaders can become prisoners to fundraising crises. We treat prospects and donors as checkbooks instead of whole persons, granting them unhealthy power over us. In the belief that more money will solve our most pressing organizational challenges, we over-rely on their resources and overweight their influence on our priorities and plans.

At the same time, we can enable the shared lie that our team's work is more noble, more spiritual, or more meaningful than that of our supporters—allowing ourselves false moral power over them. As our budgets grow, we may lose our wonder and gratitude for the generosity that enables us to do the work at hand, often moving from one "close" to the next.

At our worst, we grow cynical when we fail to raise the funding we seek, avoiding our own responsibility and instead passing judgment on what we perceive as the affluence or apathy of the "donor class."

We can also be tempted to isolate our donors from the messy and unpredictable world of our programs and the communities we serve. We may justify unhealthy behavior and manipulation to convince donors to support our work, bringing about a mutually assured distrust as we chase after whatever we believe will secure funding.

Instead, we long for donor relationships of mutual benefit, respect, and trust.

PRACTICES

1. Our funding relationships begin with an invitation to join our organization's community as well as its mission. As mutual trust develops, we invite potential and current funders into closer relationship. If we discern that a closer relationship is not in the organization's or potential funder's best interests, we graciously withdraw from closer contact rather than pursuing money without relationship.

2. We solicit funds based on our organization's clear and defined direction and our intended uses for the funds, based on our track record of managing the organization's finances with discipline. We don't only provide donors with the good news; instead, we appropriately share our successes, challenges, shifts in direction, and questions.

3. Our funding processes engage donors as people with needs and interests that we can serve, not only as those with resources that can serve us. We listen to their passions and aspirations, drawing them further into our work if appropriate, or joyfully introducing them to other organizations whose missions would be more aligned with their interests.

4. Where appropriate, we bring supporters to the locations of our service to help them develop a deeper understanding of the work being done. We creatively develop their interest and skill in our work, inviting them to learn together with us how to boost our impact.

5. We relate to supporters with unexpected care and respect—regularly thanking and serving them, communicating the impact of their support, and finding appropriate moments of celebration.

6. We invest in the people, systems, and long-term fundraising strategies that inspire confidence in our mission, support thoughtful donor experiences, and allow us to avoid desperate appeals.

THE GOOD NEWS

As stewards of our organization's resources, we are free to rest in the assurance that God will provide the resources the mission needs. While we work with creativity and tenacity to encourage donors to give, we are relaxed and open-handed about the outcome of each proposal. We take a long view of our relationship with each supporter, which opens space for genuine friendships.

We experience the relief and mutuality that comes from telling an integrated story to our donors. We lay down much of the burden of anxiety over our organizational performance in the presence of supporters. Instead, we can see them as true partners, sharing that burden and working shoulder-to-shoulder toward the same goals.

We demonstrate and experience the power of the gospel as we subvert the predominant narrative of scarcity in our sector. We prove that we can be trusted with little or with much. We open new possibilities for abundance, collaboration, and impact as we bless funders and other agencies by connecting them with one another.

Having invested in capable fundraising teams and processes, we can be freed from the anxiety of fixating on transactional, last-minute appeals; instead, we experience the joy of cultivating donor relationships whose financial involvement may ebb and flow over time.

Our team members benefit from the chance to experience God's good provision in times of shortfall and plenty. The people we serve can participate with dignity and mutuality in humanizing encounters and relationships with people of greater means.

IDENTITY

WE SURRENDER OUR IDENTITY TO GOD

SUMMARY

We surrender our identity to God and our ambition to the good of our neighbors. Instead of acting as though we own the organization, we practice the mindsets and habits of stewardship, using our position to advance others' glory and fullness rather than our own.

OUR REALITY

As leaders we begin with a burning sense of calling to the people we serve, attuned to God's heart for the issues and communities at the center of our mission. Even when the work is hard and slow, we flourish in the satisfactions of pioneering new work: seemingly inexhaustible stores of energy for the mission; rapid learning curves; authorship of an organizational narrative; innovation and design in problem solving and model building; solidarity with others in the effort. We can bear witness to the power of God working through our imagination and leadership.

As enterprising leaders, though constrained externally in various ways, we make every meaningful decision about what the venture does and does not do. In many respects, especially in early stages, our personal character is the ethical rudder of the organization. Our imagination is the vector of the organization's innovation. Our ambition is the index of the organization's appetite for scale. This level of agency is daunting, though exhilarating.

Over time, the challenges of nonprofit leadership compound. We may experience setbacks in our programs; alienation from certain people we serve; the departure of trusted co-laborers; the burden of funding a growing organization in an environment of apparent scarcity. Resentment can build among our closest family and friends, as we struggle to make time for all our priorities. Without noticing it, we become more susceptible to the nobility trap.

As our organization grows and we can no longer personally integrate all functions and relationships, we make our peace with the stakeholder gap. We learn to take satisfaction in sharing leadership, yet in trying moments we may feel that our ambition and vision—the generative fuel of the mission—is being thwarted. The state of our funding campaigns feels like a referendum on our worth as a leader. For better and (mostly) for worse, our stewardship mentality gradually tightens into an ownership mentality, and our belief in the mission becomes inextricable from our belief in ourselves.

The heart of this conflict is a distortion of our identity relative to the mission and organization. We "know" that our true identity rests in Christ and not in our association with this nonprofit. We "know" that we are stewards and not owners of the mission. We "know" that our ambition must be surrendered to God's purposes.

But in our hearts and through our leadership we act out the world's dominant script, which assures nonprofit leaders of their virtue in doing good, admires them for overworking, applauds them for driving growth, bids them to hold the stage, and reinforces the dangerous link between personal brand and mission brand.

Instead, we long for God's love to define our identity so that we can surrender our ambition to him.

PRACTICES

1. We use our power wisely and courageously for the sake of our team and mission, and not for our own benefit. As we take calculated risks to increase the organization's impact, we willingly absorb the downside vulnerability of these risks, and generously share the upside credit with our team. We create ways for our team members to glean opportunities for growth and satisfaction that might otherwise be ours—for example, delegating not merely the tasks and roles we don't enjoy, but also those that we prefer to do ourselves.

2. Understanding that our zeal for growth and impact puts pressure on the organization, we seek redemptive ways to relieve the unhelpful aspects of that pressure. Before we set and commit the organization to ambitious goals, we involve the people who must work to meet those goals. We bring our most consequential decisions before God and each other—not making decisions by committee, but informing them through community.

3. We practice "dispensability," setting patterns as early as possible in the life of our organization that acknowledge our limits and demonstrate that the mission can advance without us. We actively counteract the temptation to inflate our personal brand by moderating our participation in the privileges of visibility, such as public speaking or writing engagements. Recognizing that we will be frequently treated as experts, we position ourselves as learners in and beyond the organization.

4. We model parity and balance in work expectations across the levels of the team. As leaders we regularly make ourselves unavailable from work and our team; we regulate our travel commitments; and we pitch in to support the teams and individuals where the need is greatest. We create space for all others to do the same, ensuring that we and the other leaders set a sustainable pace, neither overworking nor avoiding their share of the burden during peak periods.

5. We make ourselves accountable to our team and board, asking searching questions and attending carefully to feedback on our leadership. We also cultivate thick relationships outside work where we can submit ourselves transparently to wise counsel, grace, and truth.

6. We consider reading and personally practicing Praxis' *A Rule of Life for Redemptive Entrepreneurs* to reinforce our identity of surrender and stewardship, and to maximize our organization's redemptive possibility.

THE GOOD NEWS

The redemptive pattern of creative restoration through sacrifice applies not only to the organization's mission but also to the leader's standing. It takes a counterintuitive, sacrificial, and sustained release of the leader's prerogatives for their leadership to have the most lasting influence.

We are persistently building an identity that is beyond the work of our organization, knowing that at some point in the future, whether by design or by default, the organization will no longer be ours to steward. As we practice our unshakable identity in Christ, he will redirect our ambition away from our own glory and toward the health of the organization and its stakeholders. We will be set free to lead from the redemptive paradox of high ambition and full surrender.

We will replenish our energy through sustainable rhythms of work and rest, and re-learn how to learn from others.

We will delight in sharing the burden and privilege of leadership across the organization—liberally distributing the power to create, to define, to decide, to care, to act.

We will recapture a healthy tolerance for risk, caring intensely and acting boldly, knowing that the grace we have been given produces faith and not certainty. As stewards rather than owners of the organization, we will experience reduced anxiety over its financial resources.

We will be poised in facing the ambiguity of our evolving role, inviting accountability from our board, peers, and trusted advisors. We will participate enthusiastically and open-handedly in succession planning, energized by the vision of an organization that endures beyond our involvement.

APPENDIX: A RULE OF LIFE FOR REDEMPTIVE ENTREPRENEURS

TIME

Instead of endless productivity, we practice a rhythm of work and rest, attending to our need to grow in all the dimensions of being human: heart, soul, mind, and strength. We commit to take one full day every week for complete rest from our daily work, and to make Sabbath possible for everyone within our sphere of authority.

MONEY

Instead of being preoccupied with money and possessions, we practice simplicity and generosity. We commit to give away a minimum of 10% of our gross income, with special attention to the needs of the materially poor.

IMAGINATION

Instead of having our imagination saturated by media, we seek to be transformed by the renewing of our mind. We commit to establish structured limits for our use of screens and our consumption of entertainment, in quantity, frequency, and moral character.

For the full Rule of Life for Redemptive Entrepreneurs: rule.praxislabs.org

DECISION-MAKING

Instead of willful autonomy in decision making, we practice active dependence on God. We commit to daily prayer, and at times of major decisions, not proceeding until we have actively submitted our own desires fully to the will of God and have inner peace about the decision.

POWER

Instead of accumulating power to benefit ourselves or exploit others, we use it to generate possibility for those who have less access to opportunity. We commit to the practice of gleaning — frequently sacrificing opportunities for our own advancement to intentionally create pathways for others. We also practice chastity and fidelity, honoring the men and women with whom we work.

COMMUNITY

Instead of individualism and isolation, we practice real presence with others who are not part of our daily work. We pursue diversity across class and ethnicity in our friendships and mentoring relationships.

This book was authored by Praxis Partners Dave Blanchard, Andy Crouch, Scott Kauffmann, and Jena Lee Nardella, and Venture Partner Peter Greer.

Our goal has been to identify the redemptive practices of the real-life nonprofits led by members of the Praxis community and beyond. Thanks to all of them, including those who reviewed early drafts, for their faithful and visionary work.

Praxis is a creative engine for redemptive entrepreneurship, supporting founders, funders, and innovators motivated by their faith to love their neighbors and renew culture.

redemptivenonprofit.org
praxislabs.org

Made in the USA
Columbia, SC
01 October 2021

46441877R00046